The Allotment

A Play

Gillian Plowman

A SAMUEL FRENCH ACTING EDITION

FOUNDED 1830

SAMUELFRENCH-LONDON.CO.UK
SAMUELFRENCH.COM

THE ALLOTMENT

First performed by Runnymede Drama Group at the Rhoda McGaw Theatre, Woking on October 6th 2004 with the following cast:

Marcie	Jill Payne
Norah	Jane Walters
Belle	Linda Russell
Lorna	Frankie Godliman
Daisy Barnes	Nicola Cutliffe

Directed by Judith Dolley
Stage-managed by Clare Pinnock
Designed by John Godliman
Lighting by Bill Payne
Sound by Ian Santry

CHARACTERS

Marcie, convicted of dangerous driving; 70
Norah, serial shoplifter; 65
Belle, PA, neat and well-groomed; 50s
Lorna, actress/singer; 56
Daisy Barnes, new probation officer; 41

Other plays by
Gillian Plowman
published by Samuel French Ltd

Beata Beatrix
Close to Croydon
David's Birthday
Janna Years
A Kind of Vesuvius
Me and My Friend
Philip and Rowena
There's None So Blind
Tippers
Touching Tomorrow
Two Fat Men
Two Summers
Umjana Land

For
Rob and Alys

THE ALLOTMENT

SCENE 1

An allotment. Summer morning

A shed sits US. There is a trellis with roses on it. The place is somewhat chaotic and there is still some digging to be done. There are various vegetables growing including carrots, peas and potatoes. There are four various tatty fold-up garden chairs and a wheelbarrow. Gardening tools and gloves have been downed. There is a tray with three teacups and a teapot and there is a signing-in book

The sound of birdsong

Women are serving community punishment orders and are growing the vegetables for soup kitchens. They are dressed for work in ways to suit their characters

Marcie, seventy, is convicted of dangerous driving. She ran over her husband. She wears trousers with many pockets containing all her necessaries. She is smoking a spliff and carries a trug

Norah is sixty-five and hasn't recovered from the death of her daughter thirty years ago. She is a serial shoplifter

Lorna is fifty-six, an actress and singer, convicted of criminal damage to the theatre where she no longer performs. She wears a glorious hat to protect her skin and is standing in the wheelbarrow holding a cup of tea

*Marcie crosses the stage purposefully to Norah, who pours a cup of
tea for herself and Marcie*

Marcie Is it Monday?
Norah No, it's Wednesday. And it's tea break.
Marcie What happened to Tuesday?
Norah Decided against it.
Marcie I'll be back for me tea.

Marcie exits

Lorna   "The crow doth sing as sweetly as the lark
                     When neither is attended, and I think
                     The nightingale, if she should sing by day,
                     When every goose is cackling, would be thought
                     No better a musician than the wren."

Marcie returns

Norah I've got a headache.
Marcie You shouldn't have — missing Tuesday.
Norah It's the sun.
Lorna Wear a hat.
Norah Haven't got a hat.
Marcie Have a puff.
Norah Makes it worse.
Marcie It's medicinal.
Norah Are you sure it's what you think it is?
Lorna   "How many things by season seasoned are
                     To their right praise and true perfection!"
Marcie Now that's true perfection. (*She produces a very small but
    perfectly formed freshly-dug carrot*)
Norah Well done!
Marcie Yes!
Lorna My hat is yours for the duration of the day.
Marcie The whole row's come up!
Lorna If you could but assist my alighting from this barrow.

Norah Are you still rehearsing?
Lorna No, I want a hand.

They hold the wheelbarrow whilst Lorna gets out

(*Of the carrot*) It's a bit small.
Marcie Yes, it's small. It's small. So were you once. You have to thin some out so that the others will have room to grow.
Norah She's not saying that's what happened to you, Lorna …
Lorna But I have been thinned out, haven't I? (*She gives the hat to Norah*)
Marcie And you can check for diseases at the same time. Want to taste it?
Norah Wait for Belle. Thank you, Lorna. Who were you doing?
Lorna Portia. From *The Merchant of Venice*. I'm on tonight. Six week run at the Playhouse. Do you want tickets? I could get you a couple each.
Norah I could take my daughter, Alice. She deserves a night out.
Lorna Opening night tonight — there'll be bouquets, champagne …
Marcie I could come tonight. Maurice loves champagne. Well, I do.
Lorna I do.
Norah I do.
Marcie I could take him a rose for his buttonhole. (*She cuts a rose from the trellis*)
Lorna Silly to cut it now, Marcie. It'll be dead by the time you get home.
Marcie Like him! No! Not like him. I'll cut another one later. He's such a dear sweet husband. Is it Shakespeare again?
Lorna Yes, I'm doing a musical after that.
Marcie He likes Shakespeare.
Norah Alice does.
Lorna How many has she got now then?
Norah Just had her third. All girls. Isn't that wonderful? Violet, Lavender and Rose.
Marcie Very smelly, babies.

Norah Scented.
Lorna You can't bring them to the theatre, scented or not.
Norah I'll get a babysitter. Could you baby-sit, Marcie, if you're
     going tonight and I'm going on Saturday?
Marcie Are you going on Saturday?
Norah If you can baby-sit.
Marcie You'll have to be back by half-past ten.
Norah Why?
Marcie 'Cos.
Norah 'Cos what?
Marcie You know.
Norah What?
Lorna Depends on the number of curtain calls.
Marcie The ...
Norah What?
Marcie (*quickly*) Curfew.
Norah Course I'll be back by then.

*Belle enters. She is aged in her fifties and is a PA. She is convicted
of blackmailing her boss, who had spurned her for a younger
secretary. She is neat and well-groomed*

Belle She's gone! She's gone!

*Norah pours a cup of tea. Marcie cuts the small carrot into four
pieces*

     I had my meeting with the new one. We got rid of her! The cow!
Marcie Bitch.
Norah Dragon.
Lorna Prima donna!
Belle Have you got a headache?
Norah It's lifting with the feathers.
Marcie Where did she go?
Belle They won't say. I said we'd like to send a card, you know from
     us on the allotment.
Norah No, we wouldn't.
Belle No, we wouldn't. It was a way of finding out what happened
     to her.

Lorna They realized that she was in danger of being buried alive.
(*She points to a shovel*)
Belle But we can still get the Rotavator.
Norah What's the new one like?
Belle You'll find out. She's coming this morning.
Norah This morning?
Marcie Baby carrot. (*She hands round the pieces of carrot*)
Norah Oh tasty.
Belle Bit small.
Marcie It's not the size that matters.
Belle No. Tasty. I just wish it was bigger because it's so tasty.
Marcie I'll thin out some more and you can have one each.

Marcie exits

Belle God, what's she smoking now — her lips have gone green.
Lorna Gangrene?
Belle Gone green.
Norah She thinks it's grass when actually it's grass.
Lorna Or spinach.
Belle God, look at my nails.

They look at her nails. Belle puts her hands behind her back

Don't look at them.
Lorna Have you had a manicure?
Belle Yes. Yes. Guess what she's done on them this time.
Norah Twirls?
Lorna Stars?
Belle My name. On each hand. (*She raises the thumb and fingers
on both hands as she says each letter*) B ... E ... L ... L ... E
Norah Pink?
Lorna Purple.
Belle Both. Pink with purple letters and little flowers coming out
of them. David loved my nails. Even when I was blackmailing
him.

Beat

Lorna There's something wrong with my hearing. (*She touches her ears*)

Norah We didn't hear that.

Belle God, sorry. It's the new one. Call me Daisy, she says. You'll see — she makes you — you know.

Lorna No.

Norah No.

Lorna What does she make you?

Belle You know.

Norah No.

Belle Talk.

Norah Oh, Belle …

Belle You don't need tits to flirt, David says. I just put my hand on the arm of a new client, you know, leading them to David's office and they look down and see my nails and well, David says, they're half way there. Can't resist the pull, like I'm not really pulling them, but they feel — wanted — drawn in. And they sign up! David says he can't do business without me. Can't do without me. (*She shows them her miserable nails*) Look at them.

Lorna They're all right. (*Singing to the tune of "Tragedy" by the Bee Gees*) Sexy nails.

Norah catches on; she sings a la-la accompaniment and jigs

(*Singing*) Sexy nails.

All three sing the la-la accompaniment and jig

Belle Look! My pods are getting fatter! They've got peas in! (*She inspects the peas*)

Lorna (*singing to the same tune*) Fatter peas.

They jig and sing another la-la accompaniment

All (*singing*) Fatter peas …

Belle It must have been the rain yesterday. (*She takes her gloves out and inspects the holes in them*)

Lorna   "The quality of mercy is not strain'd."
Belle The quality of my gloves leaves a lot to be desired.

Lorna climbs back into the barrow and makes the following speech beautifully. The others listen as they work

Lorna   "It droppeth as the gentle rain from heaven
                   Upon the place beneath: it is twice blessed;
                   It blesses him that gives and him that takes:
                   'Tis mightiest in the mightiest: it becomes
                   The thronèd monarch better than its crown;
                   His sceptre shows the force of temporal power
                   The ..." (*She stops*)
Belle That's beautiful.
Norah It's her opening night tonight.
Lorna I can't remember any more.
Norah Lorna's getting us tickets. Marcie's taking Maurice tonight
    and I'm taking Alice on Saturday. When do you and David want
    to go?
Lorna I won't be able to go on ...
Norah Yes you will.
Lorna I can't remember any more ...
Norah You'll remember it when you get there.
Lorna Yes. Do you want tickets, Belle?
Belle No.
Lorna No?
Belle Didn't you hear? Someone burnt the Playhouse down.

They are aghast

Black-out

SCENE 2

The same. Later that morning

*Daisy Barnes is the new probation officer monitoring the women.
She is forty-one. She carries files and has the rose Marcie picked
earlier. Marcie is working*

Marcie Me carrots is coming on a treat. I've got spuds, cabbages,
   them little marrows ...
Daisy Courgettes.
Marcie Them. And — beetroot.
Daisy Excellent. That's truly excellent. All good stuff for the soup
   kitchen.
Marcie What happened to her then? She went suddenly, didn't she?
   We didn't like her. Too strict.
Dasiy You're not on holiday, you know.
Marcie I'm seventy. I shouldn't be doing this hard work.
Daisy What did you expect to be doing?
Marcie People of seventy should be looked after.
Daisy I'm here to look after you all. This is beautiful, thank you.
   Where are the others?
Marcie On a mission.
Daisy What mission?
Marcie I dunno what. If they're not here, they must be on a mission,
   mustn't they?
Daisy Didn't they say?
Marcie I was doin' me carrots. We only talk in tea break you know,
   unless it's "Can I borrow your spade?" or "What the hell's that?"
   when something weird has popped up amongst your cabbages.
   You find bones and all sorts. There's bodies been buried here you
   know. It wasn't a plague pit, was it?
Daisy I don't know. Have they been here at all this morning?

Marcie hands the signing-in book to Daisy

Marcie Signed in. Belladonna was late but she had to go to the
   manicurist first.

Daisy looks at the book

Daisy She came to see me.

Marcie Could you have a go at my nails? They've split.

Daisy I'm your new probation officer and I told Belle to say that I was coming this morning for a group supervision session. Didn't she tell you?

Marcie I knew you were coming. That's why I picked the rose.

Daisy Very thoughtful of you.

Marcie I'm a thoughtful person.

Daisy Are you?

Marcie Maurice is away on a business trip and I'm doing the garden whilst he's away. That's thoughtful.

Daisy Maurice is ... ?

Marcie My husband.

Daisy I've got your notes here. Marcelle Pinkerton.

Marcie Marcie's fine.

Daisy And you live ... ?

Marcie At home. With Maurice.

Daisy How long have you and Maurice been married?

Marcie Forty-seven years. Getting everything in trim for our golden.

Daisy And home is ... ?

Marcie Where the heart is.

Daisy I've got your address as Vine Road Hostel.

Beat

Marcie I stay over when I'm working. He leaves me to do everything, Maurice. I can smoke, can't I?

Daisy I'd rather you didn't but I can't stop you.

Marcie I roll me own. (*She takes her grass from one of her many pockets and starts to roll*)

Daisy What's that?

Marcie It's not what you think it is. You need a greenhouse for that.

Daisy Would you like a greenhouse?

Marcie I would!

Daisy I could put something in the local paper — see if anyone's got one they don't want.

Marcie This is just — a weed.

Daisy I can't let you smoke weeds — you could be harming yourself. (*She holds out her hand*)

Marcie puts the roll-up back in her pocket

Marcie I think people should be allowed to harm themselves at seventy. Do themselves in, if you like. Too many old people. What's the point of them?

Daisy Their wisdom and experience has a lot to contribute to society.

Marcie Only if people will listen to them. Do you find anyone under twenty wants to listen to you?

Daisy They have to listen to me if they're on probation. I've spent the last ten years dealing with young offenders.

Marcie Doing what?

Daisy We have to put in place an action plan to prevent re-offending, organize training and proper work and have regular meetings to see if the plan is being stuck to. The same as we're doing here.

Marcie I haven't got an action plan.

Daisy Yes you have.

Marcie Have I?

Daisy Yes.

Marcie So what is it?

Daisy Well, you have to carry out your community punishment order of a hundred and forty hours of unpaid work, that is growing vegetables for the soup kitchen. You have to behave yourself in the hostel.

Marcie I do.

Daisy I'm told you shout a lot.

Marcie To make them listen to me.

Daisy And you take in alcohol which you're not allowed to do.

Marcie You agree with me.

Daisy What?

Marcie There's no point in living after seventy.
Daisy There will be if you have a greenhouse.
Marcie I can grow cannabis!
Daisy No, you can't grow cannabis.
Marcie I could do more things before I was seven than I can after
I'm seventy ... What's the point?
Daisy Let's look at the rest of your plan. You need to prove to the
social workers that you are capable of looking after yourself on
your own. Then they will find you somewhere where you can live
independently.
Marcie But what about Maurice?
Daisy Yes, Maurice.
Marcie He'll be expecting me back home.
Daisy I expect you miss him.
Marcie I can't get there. They've taken my car.
Daisy Yes I know. It's difficult without a car.
Marcie Who's meeting him off the train every day?

Pause

Daisy When did you last see him?
Marcie He was — lit up.
Daisy Lit up?
Marcie Standing there — lit up.
Daisy And where were you?
Marcie In the car.
Daisy And?

Long pause

Was he in the headlights of the car?
Marcie Lit up, yes. His hand was up ... (*She shades her eyes with
her hand*) And he was telling me to lower the lights. Shouting at
me.
Daisy He was shouting at you?
Marcie Nothing I do is right for Maurice. He tells me off when I'm
driving. Watches everything I do and it makes me very nervous

and I do things wrong and he shouts ... I — I ... Then one time, I
opened the door and I didn't look in the mirror and this car drove
into the door and Maurice — it could have taken my arm off but
he didn't care about that — it was the car.

Daisy Is it just when you're driving?

Marcie What?

Daisy That he shouts?

Marcie No. It's his meals. They're never right. And my friends.
And the things I watch on the telly and what I wear and my breath
smells, he says, from cigarettes.

Daisy He's difficult to live with?

Marcie No, I am. Ask Maurice.

Pause

Daisy I can't ask Maurice, can I?

Marcie stares at her and then coughs

You were in the car?

Marcie Yes.

Daisy And Maurice was in the headlights?

Marcie Yes.

Daisy And he was shouting at you?

Marcie Horrid ugly face shouting at me.

Daisy What did you think?

Marcie That for all those years, he had — always had a horrid ugly
face when he looked at me. Never a kind, smiling face. All those
years I was someone who made him horrid and ugly.

Daisy You deserved someone who smiled at you.

Marcie He deserved someone to smile at.

Daisy That's not the way to look at it.

Marcie You're frowning at me. I can't do this. I can't do that.
You're not smiling. It's me.

Daisy So what did you do?

Marcie I thought — I'd like to stop him looking at me if it makes
him so unhappy so I'll kill myself. Crash the car with me in it.

Daisy That's not what happened.

Marcie No. Whilst I was thinking about where to crash the car, my foot slipped off the clutch and I ran straight over Maurice.

Daisy You killed him.

Marcie I didn't mean to.

Daisy Maybe you did.

Marcie No. Ask Maurice. I'm a very bad driver.

Daisy I believe that it is better to face up to the truth. Only then can you leave behind the bad things in your life, wipe the slate clean, and face the future.

Marcie I was convicted of dangerous driving.

Daisy Did you mean to kill him?

Norah, Belle and Lorna enter with a Rotavator

Marcie turns to them sadly

Marcie I killed Maurice.

Lorna We've only been gone twenty minutes.

Beat

Norah And, anyway, we've just seen him.

Marcie Maurice?

Norah At the place where we got the Rotavator. He persuaded the man to let us have it for free, as it's in a good cause.

Lorna And — he said he liked my hat.

Norah He said it to me.

Lorna But it's my hat.

Norah A hat's not a hat 'til it's on a head.

Daisy Maurice is dead.

Lorna He said he liked it.

Norah On my head.

Marcie He would. He likes hats.

Belle This is Mrs Barnes.

Norah Oh.

Lorna Oh.

Daisy Call me Daisy. (*She glances at Norah — something about her rings a bell*) I'm your new probation officer. Belle and I met this morning and I've just had a one to one with Marcella.

Marcie Marcie.

Norah One to one what?

Daisy Talk. It was very productive.

They all look at Marcie

I'll be having individual meetings with you all on a regular basis of course, but I wanted to come and see where you work and well, frankly, to get to know you as a group. We'll have a group supervision session right now. Is there another seat?

Norah No.

Daisy Well, do sit down, all of you. (*She looks at her notes*)

The others sit. Dasiy looks for something to sit on. She finds a bucket which she upends and sits on

Now, Belle and Marcie, we've made a good start, I think you'll agree.

Marcie and Belle look at each other

Truth is the key. Being honest with ourselves and each other in order to make retribution and reparation.

Marcie To make what?

Daisy To pay for what we've done wrong, to make up for it.

Lorna (*deliberately*) We like the way we do it.

Daisy Lorna Gaffe?

Lorna No.

Daisy frowns and looks at Norah

Norah Not me.

Lorna Lorna Truman. My stage name.

Daisy I've got Gaffe down here.

Lorna I don't use it.
Daisy I'll use Truman then.
Lorna Right.
Daisy And Norah Hilton? Mrs Hilton?
Norah Yes.
Daisy Your second marriage?
Norah If it's relevant.
Daisy It's just — to get some background.
Norah And what about you? Background ...
Daisy I'm married. I've just come back to this area. I used to live
here when I was a child. I have a daughter who is ten. Alice ...
Marcie Like you, Norah! Norah's got a daughter; Alice.

Beat

Daisy I've been a probation officer for nearly twenty years.
Marcie She's been doing kids.
Daisy Young offenders.
Lorna And now you've got us! What are you going to do with us?
Daisy I'm going to look after you, help you to complete your
community punishment orders without going back to court, and
plan for the future. I want to be open and honest with you and I
want you to be the same with me. And with each other. Because
you are all mature ladies, and because you all have some gardening
experience, you have been given this allotment to manage without
total supervision. We trust you, and the proof of the pudding —
or the soup! — is in the eating. (*She laughs*)

The others do not laugh. There is an uncomfortable silence

(*Turning to Laura*) What is your way?
Lorna   "I never did repent for doing good,
                   Nor shall not now: for in companions
                   That do converse and waste the time together,
                   Whose souls do bear an equal yoke of love."
Marcie Shakespeare. Have you heard of him?
Daisy I have, yes. Your way, Lorna?

Lorna We can be what we like on the allotment. It is — how we
want it to be. We are good. We care for the people we choose to
have in our lives. We share them with each other. And our
vegetables grow. Don't spoil it. Would you like tickets for the
Playhouse?

Belle Yes, David and I are going.

Daisy What did you promise at our meeting this morning?

Belle That wasn't here. It's different.

Daisy Why is it different?

Belle An office. Agenda. Notes. Proposals. Minutes — very fast
shorthand. Agreeing things.

Daisy Exactly. A course of action.

Belle Making sure everyone knows. Communication is the most
difficult management tool.

Daisy So what did we agree? Belle?

Belle What?

Daisy To face the truth.

They all look at Belle

And communicate it.

Pause

Belle You can't appear at the Playhouse, Lorna. It's burnt down.

Lorna I know that. It's an open air production. In the shell of the
Playhouse. It's a very dramatic setting. But bring a blanket. Once
the sun goes down, it gets quite chilly.

Beat

Daisy Belle.

Belle We'll take a blanket.

Daisy About David.

Belle He can't come.

Daisy Why not?

Belle Something happened to him.

Daisy What happened to him?
Belle I ...
Norah Why can't he come? You go everywhere together.
Belle No ... (*She is distressed*)
Norah (*to Daisy*) You should stop all this. Look what you're doing to her.
Lorna Do it our way.
Daisy Belle.
Belle He was cheating on his wife.
Norah You don't have to do this, Belle.
Belle With a junior secretary. One of my juniors. I was in charge of three secretaries you know. None of them had nails to beat mine ... I was on my way home when I realized I'd forgotten some files I was going to work on so I came back to the office and David was making love to this junior secretary on my desk. My desk. Why my desk? Why not his desk? Or her desk? My desk! I had the firm's digital camera in my bag — I did the company newsletter, you see, so I took a photo of them — showing everything. I can't believe they didn't notice the flash. But they didn't. Car headlights flashing and street lights flashing on the windows, I suppose. And they were engrossed in what they were doing.
Marcie He was doing her? On a desk?
Belle My desk! I got up quite close and took another photo. And another. Quite a lot. Then I left. It should have been me.
Marcie If it was your desk ...
Belle I emailed him a photo the next day and asked for a thousand pounds. He came rushing round, explaining that it was me he wanted but her who offered.
Lorna What!?
Belle I sent him the next photo and asked for five thousand pounds. He confiscated my computer. I put the photos on her computer when she was out to lunch and sent him the next one, asking for another five thousand pounds. I said I would send it to everyone in the organization if he didn't pay up.
Marcie Did he?
Belle Yes.
Marcie That's eleven thousand pounds so far.

Norah Did he confiscate her computer?

Belle Yes. I said I had discs and discs of photos and could put them all on any computer in the world and he couldn't stockpile all the computers in the world in his office.

Marcie Blimey.

Belle I said if he sacked me I'd send the photos to head office. I said I'd print one out and send it to his wife and asked for another ten thousand pounds to stop me.

Marcie Did you get it?

Belle Yes but I'd put the photo in an envelope and addressed it ready and it sort of got sent. She told the police.

Marcie Are they divorced now?

Belle She forgave him and they went on a second honeymoon and I got convicted of blackmail. Where's the justice in that?

Norah No justice.

Lorna None.

Belle And I lost my job. And he's been promoted to head office. And I love him.

Marcie Did you keep the money?

Norah (*to Daisy*) What's the point of putting her through that?

Belle They didn't let me keep the money.

Daisy So that she can start to build her future.

Belle It's without him though, isn't it? I had him — on the allotment. Till you — —

Marcie I had Maurice.

Silence

Daisy Lorna?

Lorna What do you want me to say? I am an actress. I am a singer — —

Daisy What are you doing here?

Lorna Oh for goodness' sake. This is where I rehearse.

Daisy For what?

Lorna For my latest production.

Daisy Which is … ?

Lorna *The Merchant of Venice*.

Daisy No, it's not.

Lorna Yes, it is. Portia — *The Merchant of Venice*.

Daisy You're too old to play Portia.

Lorna Too old! I'm fifty-six. Is that old? Too old to play Portia. I was never without a part. Always working. Turned down three proposals of marriage so that I could carry on touring ... I don't look fifty-six, do I?

Marcie No, you don't ...

Lorna Inside I'm Juliet and Rosalind — all those theatres — now I see other names on the boards outside. They don't want me any more ...

Norah Of course they do.

Lorna Never to stand in the spotlight again.

Daisy What about the Playhouse?

Lorna If I can't play there, nobody's going to play there!

Silence

Daisy So what did you do?

Lorna It was dark. There was nobody there.

Daisy What did you do?

Lorna I set fire to it.

Pause

Daisy Criminal damage.

Silence

Lorna slowly takes her hat off and spins it into the vegetables

There are several very good amateur dramatic societies in this area who would love to have you ...

Lorna I'm a professional! (*She turns away*)

They all look at Norah

Norah Me. Eh? Me. My turn? Get it over with. Get you off our
  backs.

Pause. Daisy checks her notes

  I steal things from shops. I'm a serial shoplifter.
Daisy Why? You have a good job. You can't be short of money.
Norah Alice is. Her husband walked out. She's got three little girls
  — Violet, Lavender and Rose.

Daisy freezes

  They can't find him. What's the use of that Child Support Agency
  if they can't find him? I pay my taxes which goes to pay the people
  who run it and they're not doing anything for Alice, and Alice has
  got the children to look after so I have to buy their clothes and I
  thought why should I when nobody's making him pay so I started
  stealing clothes for them. I told them in court how they're letting
  Alice down and I'm just seeking publicity to show how they've
  failed Alice. That's why I'm stealing.

Daisy can barely speak

Daisy Where does Alice live?
Norah Lawley Street. She came to live with me, but then I moved
  to live with my new husband and they let her stay in our old house.
Daisy What is Alice's surname?
Norah She kept her own name.
Daisy What is it?
Norah Spencer.

Daisy is shaken

  All right?

Silence

Daisy stares at Norah

Daisy You shouted at me.
Norah What?
Belle She didn't. What are you talking about?
Daisy I — I ... She ... (*She shakes*) You hit me. (*She touches her cheek in memory*)
Marcie No, she didn't.
Belle Are you all right?
Daisy I ... No ...
Belle Mrs Barnes ...
Daisy It's Margaret. My name. When I was a child — when I lived here — my name was Margaret Kefford.
Norah Jesus Christ.

Norah is stunned

You knew who I was.
Daisy No. I was only ten. I didn't remember what you looked like. You've changed your name.
Norah So have you.
Lorna What is it? Norah ... ?
Norah And you called your daughter Alice.
Daisy Yes.
Norah How dare you.
Lorna Norah?
Norah How fucking dare you! (*She strikes Daisy across the face*)

Daisy stumbles and drops her files. Silence. Everyone is aghast

Daisy That's ... Maybe that's enough for today.
Norah Face the truth! Face up to reality! Put it all behind us and plan for the future. Go on then, it's your turn, Margaret Kefford, tell us what you did!
Daisy No.
Norah Worse than anything any of us have done.
Marcie What?

Norah Tell them!
Daisy No. The group work is for you.
Norah This is for me!
Belle Tell us.

They all surround Daisy

Daisy When I was ten, my best friend was Alice Spencer.
Marcie Norah's Alice!?
Daisy We did everything together. We wanted to get our map reading badge so we practised with the street map. We crept out of our houses after tea one evening to map read in the dark and — we got abducted.
Marcie What?
Daisy A car stopped and we were forced into it — two men — and ...

Norah breaks down

They kept us locked up for four days and, when they weren't there, we talked about the future, Alice and I. She said she wanted to have three little girls and she was going to call them Violet, Lavender and Rose.
Marcie She did!
Daisy And I said I would call my little girl Alice after her ... On the fourth day — Tuesday — —
Marcie Tuesday.
Daisy — we worked out a plan to escape. One of us would lie on the floor with a body that we made out of bits of carpet so it looked like two bodies and the other would hide behind the door and escape and run for help.
Norah Why you — Why you ... ?
Daisy I was always first in the school races.

Beat

It worked.
Marcie Good!
Daisy I got out and ran.

Marcie You escaped?
Daisy Yes.

Silence

Marcie And ... ?

Dasiy can't go on

Norah They killed Alice.
Belle Oh God.
Marcie Alice is dead?
Norah She left her. She ran away and left Alice to die.
Daisy I went for help!
Norah YOU LEFT ALICE TO DIE!

There is a long silence. The birds stop singing. The Lights dim as a shadow passes over them all

Lorna Norah?
Norah What?
Lorna Can you give us a hand with the Rotavator? (*She touches Norah*)

They all help with the Rotavator. Daisy doesn't move

The sun comes out and the birds twitter

Lorna retrieves her hat. Marcie lights a spliff. Norah and Belle pick up tools

Lorna   "And earthly power doth then show likest God's
                   When mercy seasons justice. Therefore, Jew,
                   Though justice be thy plea, consider this ..."
I've remembered it. Opening night tonight!
Belle (*to Daisy*) Do you want to come with David and me?
Marcie Maurice and I are going tonight.
Norah You could come Saturday with Alice and me. She'd love to
see you again.

Lorna Do it our way.

Daisy slowly picks up her files

Daisy Yes, I'll ... I'll come on Saturday. I'd like to see — Alice
again.
Marcie Lovely. I'll just pick Maurice his rose. He can wear it
tonight.
Belle I'll pick one for David. Shall we meet for a drink beforehand?
Lorna   "We do pray for mercy,
                And that same prayer doth teach us all to render
                The deeds of mercy."

Music fades in

Black-out

THE END

FURNITURE AND PROPERTY LIST

SCENE 1

On stage: Shed
Trellis with roses
Growing vegetables including carrots, peas and potatoes
Tatty fold-up garden chairs
Wheelbarrow
Various gardening tools including shovels and a bucket
Several pairs of gardening gloves
Tray with three tea-cups and teapot
Signing-in book
Trug for **Marcie**
Tea-cup for **Lorna**

Personal: **Marcie**: spliff, packet of grass, cigarette-papers, lighter, small freshly-dug carrot, secateurs
Belle: gardening gloves with holes

SCENE 2

Set: Files for **Daisy**

Off stage: Rotavator (**Norah, Belle** and **Lorna**)

LIGHTING PLOT

Practical fittings required: nil
1 exterior setting. The same throughout

SCENE 1 Summer

To open: Exterior morning light; sunshine

| *Cue* 1 | They all look aghast | (Page 7) |
| | *Black-out* | |

SCENE 2 Later that morning

To open: Exterior morning light; sunshine

| *Cue* 2 | **Norah:** "YOU LEFT ALICE TO DIE!" | (Page 23) |
| | *Darken lighting; shadow effect* | |

| *Cue* 3 | **All**, except **Daisy**, help with the Rotavator | (Page 23) |
| | *Revert to bright sunshine* | |

| *Cue* 4 | Music fades in | (Page 24) |
| | *Black-out* | |

EFFECTS PLOT

SCENE 1

Cue 1   To open   (Page 1)
          Birdsong, continuous throughout

SCENE 2

Cue 2   To open   (Page 8)
          Birdsong, continuous

Cue 3   **Norah**: "YOU LEFT ALICE TO DIE!"   (Page 23)
          Cut birdsong

Cue 4   **All**, except **Daisy**, help with the Rotavator   (Page 23)
          Twittering birdsong

Cue 5   **Lorna**: " 'The deeds of mercy.'"   (Page 24)
          Music

Printed by The Kingfisher Press, London NW10 7AS